PRACTICAL KARATE:

FOR WOMEN

A Guide to Everyman's Self-defense . . . .

CHARLES E. TUTTLE COMPANY: PUBLISHERS
Tokyo, Japan & Rutland, Vermont

PRACTICAL KARATE:

FOR WOMEN

by
M. Nakayama
&
Donn F. Draeger

BOOK V

Representatives

For Continental Europe:
BOXERBOOKS, INC., Zurich

For the British Isles:
PRENTICE-HALL INTERNATIONAL, INC., London

For Canada:
HURTIG PUBLISHERS, Edmonton

For Australasia:
BOOK WISE (AUSTRALIA) PTY. LTD.
104–108, Sussex Street, Sydney 2000

Published by the Charles E. Tuttle Company, Inc.
of Rutland, Vermont and Tokyo, Japan
with editorial offices at Suido 1-chome, 2–6
Bunkyo-ku, Tokyo, Japan

Library of Congress Catalog Card No. 65–12268

International Standard Book No. 0-8048-0485-0

First edition, 1965
Seventh printing, 1977

Layout and typography by
Keiko Chiba

Printed in Japan

TABLE OF CONTENTS

AUTHORS' FOREWORD

THIS book is *for* you, the ladies, not about you. Please accept it in its intended constructive purpose. It has the very difficult task of bringing to you safe, workable self-defense *karate* responses for standing positions against a single assailant without requiring you engage in the severe discipline of, and dedication to, daily training required by classical *karate*. It is not however, an exhaustive survey of *karate* methods, but chooses those which give direct consideration to easy learning for the average female.

You may find this book overly frank and you may be a bit shocked at its approach. Read it anyway for this approach can save your virtue or life. . . . or *both*!

Whether you are beautiful or plain, you are not immune from attacks against your person. There is likewise no guarantee that your name will not join tomorrow's multitude of crime statistics recorded in the daily papers. Police files are filled with an ever increasing number of assaults, robberies, rapes, and other vicious attacks committed against women. Less serious, but nevertheless objectionable, are the operations of "mashers" and meddlesome males who molest women and girls in urban areas. You need to develop a skill with a system of self-defense, whether you are a housewife, student, career girl, or a lady of leisure.

We are dismayed to see that the recent *karate* boom around the world has given a lucrative chance for unscrupulous and unqualified self-appointed *karate* "experts" to prey on innocent and unsuspecting women. Many of these "experts" who are not qualified to properly instruct in such a serious subject as self-defense for women, offer

7

short courses in self-defense mastery that promise complete safety under any and all circumstances if only the subscriber will pay to learn certain Oriental secrets. False confidence, established as a result of these teachings, can cause, when brought to the test, endless misery and even disaster. Authentic *karate* teachers do reside abroad and their teachings have full merit, but choose your instructor carefully, for your very life is in his hands. *Karate* techniques properly taught, will be an invaluable tool of self-defense for the rest of your life. Badly taught technique may hospitalize you. . . . or *bury* you.

This book, like its predecessors, is a categorized collection of self-defense situations and recommended *karate* responses which will better prepare you for emergencies should defense of your property, virtue, or your life become necessary. *Karate* responses for women *can be* precisely these applied by the male sex, but, more often than not, modifications are required to ensure the success of the defense. The fundamentals described in Book One of this series hold true and should be practiced, but basic physiological differences in your female body and the lack of the ability to generate sufficient functional strength required for some of these male responses should be borne in mind. Further, limitations on movement imposed by female wearing apparel (high heels, tight skirts) cancel out much useful *karate* technique, and it must be modified accordingly.

It is not necessary to wait until you have practiced all the fundamentals of Book One before going on to the self-defense situations in this book. You may, with a minimum of practice of the fundamentals required for these situations of your choice, practice the situations and responses until you have an efficient working knowledge. Use Book One as a reference as you go step-by-step through the various situations in this book.

You are reminded that even mastery of what is contained in this text *will not* make you invincible in personal encounters, and that mere reading with one or two rehearsals of each response in this book will not produce effective results.

The authors are indebted to the Japan Karate Association, Tokyo, Japan, for the use of their facilities, and hereby acknowledge with pleasure the assistance of those members and officials who have made this book possible. Additional thanks are due to Kazuo Obata, whose excellent photographic skills have contributed greatly towards the easy readability of this book; to —— for her posing as the "victim"; and to George Hoff, a student of combative arts, whose realistic posing for the "assailant" part of this text is highly professional.

Tokyo, Japan

M. NAKAYAMA

DONN F. DRAEGER

PREFACE

KARATE is a martial art developed by people who were prohibited the use of weapons, thus making it a *defensive* art. When one is attacked, the empty hands (which the word *karate* implies) are quite sufficient to defend oneself if one is highly skilled in the art. However, to become highly skilled takes exacting discipline, both mental and physical. The main purpose of this series of six books is to avoid the advanced techniques of *karate* which require many years of study and instead to describe simplified *karate* technique as easy-to-learn responses to typical self-defense situations.

Karate is highly esteemed as a sport, self-defense, and as a physical attribute for athletics in general. It is becoming increasingly popular in schools, offices, factories, law enforcement agencies and the armed services, varying in degree as required by the respective wants and needs.

In response to the many requests for treatment of *karate* purely as a defensive system, it is hoped that the information contained in this series of six books will be more than sufficient to meet these requests. In conclusion, if readers of this series of books will fully understand the principles and ideals of *karate*, taking care to use its techniques with discretion, they will reflect great credit to this magnificent art.

ZENTARO KOSAKA
Former Foreign Minister
of Japan
Director, Japan Karate Association

THE FIRST and most complete and authoritative text on *karate* in the English language, titled *Karate: The Art of "Empty Hand" Fighting,* by Hidetaka Nishiyama and Richard C. Brown, instructor and member of the Japan Karate Association respectively, made its appearance in 1960. It presents *karate* in its three main aspects—a healthful physical art, an exciting sport, and an effective form of self-defense. As such, it is considered the standard textbook of the Japan Karate Association and adequately serves both as a reference and instructional manual for novice and expert alike.

Many students of *karate* find the study of classical *karate* somewhat impractical in modern Western society, chiefly because time limitations prohibit sufficient practice. These students generally desire to limit their interpretations of *karate* to self-defense aspects. With this sole training objective in mind, a series of six books is being prepared which describes in simplified form the necessary *karate* movements for personal defense that can be learned by anybody of average physical abilities.

The authors, Mr. Nakayama, Chief Instructor of the Japan Karate Association and Donn F. Draeger, a well-known instructor of combative arts, bring a balanced, practical, and functional approach to *karate*, based on the needs of Western society. As a specialized series of *karate* texts, these are authentic books giving full and minute explanations of the practical art of self-defense. All movements are performed in normal daily dress and bring the performer closer to reality.

Today, *karate* is attracting the attention of the whole world and is being popularized at an amazing rate. I sincerely hope that this series of books will be widely read as a useful reference for the lovers of *karate* all over the world. It is further hoped that the techniques shown in this series of books need never be used by any reader, but should an emergency arise making their use unavoidable, discretion in application should be the keynote.

MASATOMO TAKAGI
Standing Director and
Head of the General Affairs
Department of the Japan
Karate Association

PRACTICAL KARATE:
FOR WOMEN

ESSENTIAL POINTS

1. Never underestimate your assailant. Always assume he is dangerous.

2. Stepping, weight shifting, and body turning are the keys to avoiding an assailant's attack and bringing him into position for your counterattack.

3. Turn your body as a unit, not in isolated parts, for maximum effect.

4. If the ground is rough, bumpy, or slick, you may be unable to maneuver as you would like. Simple weight shifting and twisting of your hips may be all that is possible. Don't get too fancy in your footwork.

5. Your body can only act efficiently in *karate* techniques if you make it a stable foundation, working from braced feet and a balanced position as you deliver your blow.

6. Coordinate your blocking or striking action to the assailant's target area with your stepping, weight shifting, and body turning for maximum effect.

7. Do not oppose superior power with power, but seek to harmonize it with your body action and direct it to your advantage.

8. Seek to deliver your striking actions to the assailant's anatomical weak points (vital points) rather than to hard, resistant areas.

9. After delivering the striking action to your assailant's target area, you must never loose sight of him and you should be constantly alert for a continuation of his attack.

10. Use discretion in dealing out punishment to any assailant. Fit the degree of punishment to the situation.

$1.00

$1.00

CAR AND DRIVER®

MAGAZINE

AT PARTICIPATING RETAILERS

SB

CONSUMER: Coupon good for $1.00 off the purchase of the November 1993 issue of CAR AND DRIVER magazine. Offer expires November 16, 1993. LIMIT ONE COUPON PER PURCHASE. Coupon not transferable. Consumer pays any sales tax. Good only in U.S.A., APO's & FPO's. Void where prohibited or restricted. Any other use constitutes fraud. **RETAILER:** To receive face value plus 8¢ handling, send to: Car and Driver, P.O. Box 880074, El Paso, TX 88588-0074. Coupon must be redeemed in compliance with this offer. Cash value 1/100¢.

$1.00

Pick Up Your Copy

Chapter One
SIMPLE HAND AND WRIST SEIZURES

THE lone male "animal" who molests and attacks a female by simple hand or wrist seizures does so for various purposes that include plain anger, robbery, or sexual lust for her bodily charms. Often these simple attacks are aimed only at restraint of the victim and develop into nothing more serious, but they can also involve follow-up actions of a serious nature which include slapping, searching, liberties with her body, punching or striking, and even kneeing or kicking. Often combinations of these methods are used until the intended object of the attack is gained, or the attack effectively stopped.

Self-defense situations which involve you with an unarmed, single male assailant, using these tactics against you in a standing position, are obviously all delicate situations in which an improper response by you may bring serious injury to you or perhaps the loss of your life.

Women highly trained in *karate* technique, though few, are able to face situations like these with a high degree of confidence, yet the difference between the highly trained female *karate* expert and you, an average woman, is great. The situations and the appropriate responses thereto shown in this chapter have been specially selected for the average woman and cover the necessary principles to deal successfully with common eventualities connected with unarmed single-assailant attacks in standing positions.

Practice all the responses with a partner. During your initial practices, begin slowly and gradually increase the speed of the "attack" and your response. Seek to build *automatic* responses. If you will practice a few minutes a day, several days a week, this development will be greatly aided.

Perform all your actions in normal daily dress. Do not make the mistake of practicing only on a smooth, flat surface such as a gym floor, but try to make these responses on grass, gravel, paved and unpaved surfaces. This will bring you closer to reality—the situations as they could really happen.

The responses of this chapter are given in terms of one side, either on the right or left, but in most instances the other side may and should be learned by simply reversing the instructions.

Finally, some advice concerning your execution of the responses. Figure on getting only *one* chance at making a response to your assailant's attack. It must therefore be effective! You should of course remain constantly alert. This enables you to attack successively, if necessary, which works in your favor toward escape, but don't fail to put *everything you have* into the first response. Of most importance is your sense of timing, that is, choosing the correct moment to go into action. This depends a lot upon the circumstances under which the attack against you is being made. An impulsive attack, for whatever objective, gives you no time to "sweet talk" yourself out of trouble or to think about what you must do. You will have to react immediately at his grasp before the situation becomes more violent. The "soft" approach is made by an assailant because he believes he can convince you that his advances will please you or there is no need to fear him as long as you cooperate. *Give the assailant what he wants!* "Cooperate" with him. You may even act a bit coy, but don't overdo it. Lead him to believe that he has sold you with his charming approach. Nothing will be more unbalancing to him than to find your soft, yielding self suddenly explode into a package of dynamite into his vital anatomical areas. In this connection, premature actions on your part, such as tugging and flailing wildly or screaming, are useful only when used correctly. They work best when other persons are nearby and can come to your rescue. If you are alone with him, keep your composure at his attack.

Drop ordinary objects you may be carrying as you go into action, whether packages from the store or your purse. Keeping things in your hands as you perform the responses is foolish. Look at it this way, sister; are these objects as precious as your health? Break or not, let them drop. Throwing objects at the assailant is generally useless unless these objects are particularly hard or sharp. While this book does not discuss the use of objects as weapons against your assailant, we encourage you to use every opportunity to employ anything and everything you can. Especially useful is the heel of your shoe used as a club in your hand, an umbrella, a sharp key or comb, a compact, a heavy book, or any one of many common household items that may be handy. Another thing, sister; unless you can qualify for the Olympic team in track and field or other sporting endeavors, your physical strength is *far below* that of the average male. This means that the use of your fist to areas such as the male mid-section won't stop any assailant, may not slow him down, and may just anger him and make him more determined. If you must use your fist, aim for his groin or facial area where your strength can take good effect. The heel of your hand or finger tips jabbed into facial areas is equally effective as is the use of your finger nails for scratching. Make a lot of use of your knee and learn to use the heel and tip of your shoe as suggested in the text. These are powerful weapons. Never drop to the ground *voluntarily*. If you are knocked down, get up quickly. A seated or reclining position can also work against you. Break away from your assailant as quickly as you can after striking. Use your imagination study to determine target areas other than the recommended responses in this chapter.

FRONTAL SINGLE ARM-SINGLE WRIST
SEIZURE (level ground and elevated position)

Situation: An assailant has grasped your right wrist from the front with his left hand. He is not pushing or pulling you, but insists on merely holding you. You have plenty of room to move around.

Response 1: At his grasp, keep your composure and balance. If it is a firm grasp, do not tug to release your captured right wrist. Rather keep it in place as you shift your weight to your slightly bent left leg. Quickly raise your right thigh parallel to the ground and whip a hard snap kick to the assailant's knee or shin of his advanced leg (left shown), using the point of your right shoe or the ball of that foot. Immediately withdraw your kicking foot, bringing your right thigh parallel to the ground as you draw your left hand to your left hip, forming a tight fist, knuckles downward. (See pictures above.)

Step forward with your right foot directly between the assailant's feet, pivoting a bit to your left so that your feet point in that direction. Simultaneously with this stepping, twist your body to your left and begin to drive your right elbow forward as you pull your right fist downward and in toward your body. (See diagram and pictures above.) This action loosens the assailant's grasp as you deliver a hard Elbow Forward Strike, using your right elbow, to the assailant's midsection, and withdraw your left arm along your left side, hand held in a tight fist, knuckle down, at your hip. This final action can be seen on the next page.

20

Response 2: If his grasp is rather gentle or loose, it is essential to keep your composure and balance. Do not tug prematurely to release your captured right wrist, but quietly take a stance somewhat wider than normal with your left foot well to the rear and at approximately right angles to your right foot. Quickly shift your weight to your left leg and slide your right foot back a short distance as shown in the diagram, being careful not to bring your feet together. As you move, make a tight fist of your captured right hand. Pull your captured arm across the front of your body in a downward direction (in line with an extension of the assailant's left arm), rotating your wrist toward your thumb as you do this. Twist your hips to the left as you pull and keep your chin tucked in tightly. As your right arm comes free from his grasp, step your right foot back in front of or just inside of the assailant's advanced left foot. (See diagram and pictures below.) Simultaneously with this stepping, deliver a hard backhand Knifehand directly to the assailant's facial area by using your right arm swung from a point near your left hip and upward across your body. This final action can be seen on the next page.

Key points: In Response 1, it is essential to keep your captured arm in place as you kick. Drop your hips a bit as you step in to deliver your final elbow action. Be alert for continuation of the assailant's attack. In Response 2, you must not make a premature tugging for he will tighten his grasp and perhaps foil this release. When you move, combine your weight shift, retreat stepping, hip twist, and the withdrawl of your captured arm into a smooth effort. Your final striking requires these actions performed smoothly in reverse manner and order. Move away quickly from him after striking.

22

Response 3: Should your assailant take a firm grasp on your right wrist while you are in an elevated position such as on a stairway, quickly shift your weight to your high-side foot with that knee slightly bent (left shown). Tug a bit to obtain the asailant's resistance, but keep your balance. (See upper picture.)

As the assailant resists your tugging action, quickly lift your right foot and bring that thigh parallel to the ground. See lower picture.

Deliver a hard right Foot Edge directly to your assailant's knee (advanced leg), groin, or mid-section. This final action can be seen on the next page.

Key points: It is essential to keep your balance, especially as you are lifting your leg to place your kicking attack. Lean away slightly from your opponent as you kick. Be alert to use your left arm in elbow or fist actions should the assailant pull you down. Move away quickly from him after kicking.

24

FRONTAL SINGLE ARM-CROSS SINGLE
WRIST SEIZURE

Situation: A frontal assailant has captured your right wrist in a cross seizure with his right hand. He refuses to release you. You have plenty of room to move about.

Response: Keep your composure and balance at his grasp. Do not tug prematurely to release yourself. Quickly step your advanced left foot behind the assailant's right foot, bending your knee and pointing your toes inward, as you also pivot your rear right foot slightly to the right rear as shown in the diagram. Simultaneously with these actions, withdraw your captured right arm downward (in line with an extension of the assailant's right arm) with a snapping motion of your forearm. Rotate your palm upward against the assailant's thumb. Keep your elbow close to your right hip. Your weight must shift to your rear right leg and your hips twist to your right to aid your arm pull. Keep your chin tucked in as you do all this. These actions will tear you away from his grasp. (See top pictures.)

Quickly use your left arm in Pressing Block fashion against the assailant's now free right arm by using your flat hand or forearm to restrain the movement of that arm. Your right arm is withdrawn along your right side, hand formed as a tight fist, knuckles down, at your hip. (See bottom picture.)

Deliver a stinging right Elbow Forward Strike directly to your assailant's groin, mid-section, or solar plexus by shifting your weight forward and twisting your body to the left. Keep your feet in place, but allow them to pivot in the direction of your striking. This final action can be seen on the next page.

Key points: Your arm release and elbow striking action must be timed with the shift of your body weight and the twist of your body. Notice that your captured arm withdrawl requires a rotation of your right palm, upward against the assailant's right thumb. After striking, keep alert to use your right knee to attack his groin region if necessary. Move away from him as quickly as you can after striking.

28

SIDE SINGLE ARM-CROSS SINGLE WRIST SEIZURE

Situation: An assailant has seized your right wrist with his right hand in a cross fashion from your right side. He is molesting you and refuses to release you. There is plenty of room to move.

29

Response 1: Keep your composure and balance as the assailant grips you. Do not struggle to free your right wrist, but quickly shift your weight to your slightly bent left leg. Rotate your right hand around under and upward to your right as you pull your right arm toward your body with a snap. Your palm should face your front with your fingers pointing upward. Press the knife-edge of your raised right hand hard against the heel of assailant's attacking hand and rapidly bring your right thigh parallel to the ground. Stamp your right foot edge or heel hard downward into the assailant's nearest knee, shin, or instep (left shown). See pictures across the top of these two pages. The final action can be seen on page 32.

Response 2: If Response 1 fails, step your right foot close to his lead foot (left shown), with your toes pointing toward his right foot. (See diagram below.) Simultaneously, rotate your right hand upward, around under the assailant's attacking right arm until your palm faces him and you are able to counter-grip his attacking arm near his wrist. Hold your left arm along the left side of your body, hand formed in a tight fist, knuckles down, at your hip. Deliver a hard left Elbow Forward Strike straight into the assailant's midsection or groin by twisting your body to the right and face into him. Your feet pivot in place a bit to make this movement powerful. (See below pictures.) This final action can be seen on the next page.

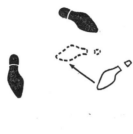

Key points: In Response 1, you must not raise your right leg preparatory to stamping until you have established some rotation of your captured hand and withdrawl of that arm. Note that this action brings the assailant's attacking arm upward and stretches it out. Press outward against it for support. In Response 2, your captured arm, after palm rotation, must pull hard downward and press against the assailant's attacking right arm to bring him forward. Coordinate your elbow striking action with the twist of your body. Be alert to use more kicking or striking if necessary. Move away from him as quickly as you can.

32

REAR SINGLE ARM-SINGLE WRIST SEIZURE

Situation: An assailant has suddenly seized your right wrist from behind you with his right hand. He is attempting to pull you backward. You have plenty of room to maneuver.

Response: At his grasp, keep your composure and balance. Step quickly backward with your left foot to a point just inside of his left foot. Point your left toes toward the left. Simultaneously with your backward step, bring your free left arm far across to the right front, hand held in a tight fist, knuckles down. See top left picture and diagram.

NOTE: If this step backward is difficult or impossible due to his strong gripping action, loosen his balance by driving a hard stamping action to the assailant's left knee, shin, or instep, using your left foot edge. (See lower left picture.)

Your backward step will bring your captured right arm around behind you in bent hammerlock fashion. Keep some strength in it by pushing your hand downward. It is good to make a tight fist with your right hand.

As you step backward, twist your hips to the left and come around fast, bringing your left Elbow Sideward Strike hard into the assailant's solar plexus, mid-section, or groin. (Upper right picture). The details of this movement can be seen from a different angle in the picture below. The final elbow action can be seen on the next page.

Key points: Blend your backward step with the pull of the assailant as he attempts to take you backward. If it is a strong pull, do not fight it at all, merely keep balance and step fast to get close in near your coming target. Your Elbow Sideward Strike must be timed with the twist of your body as you come around fast to your left. Be alert to continue with additional stamping if necessary. Break away from him as quickly as you can.

REAR SINGLE ARM-CROSS SINGLE WRIST SEIZURE

Situation: An assailant has surprised you from behind by cross-seizing your right wrist with his left hand. He only keeps you from walking away, but does not pull or push you. You have a lot of room to move about in.

Response 1: Try to break away from his grasp by simply stepping forward with your left foot and pulling your arm. He will now respond by gripping more strongly and may try to pull you back. As he does, pivot your right foot to the left and step your left foot around behind you to a position outside of and behind his left foot. (See diagram.) As you do this, bring your free left arm across your body to your right front, hand held in a tight fist, knuckles down. (See pictures top of this page.)

Simultaneously with your back step, swing your body around fast to the left and bring your left Elbow Sideward Strike hard into the rib or kidney area of your assailant's left side. (Pictures top of next page.) The final striking action can be seen at the top of page 40.

Response 2: If your assailant takes a relatively loose grasp, simply step your right foot backwards deeply between his two feet and raise your captured arm, elbow upward, hand held in a tight fist as shown in the picture to the right. Drive a hard right Elbow Sideward Strike into the assailant's solar plexus, midsection, or groin. The final action can be seen on next page, center picture.

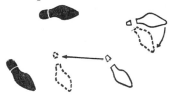

Response 3: If your assailant pushes you forward, keep balance and raise your right thigh parallel to the ground. (See bottom picture.) Stamp a hard right foot edge or heel directly into his left knee, shin, or instep. This final action can be seen on the bottom of the next page.

Key points: In Response 1, blend your step, twist, and elbow striking action into a smooth movement. In Response 2, sometimes an assailant aids you by trying to twist your arm into hammerlock position. In stepping, go to a position deep between his legs with your right foot. In Response 3, use the assailants attacking arm as a support while you deliver your stamping action. Don't lean too far away from your opponent during stamping. In all responses, be alert to use other measures should the assailant continue his attack. Move away quickly from him when he releases you.

FRONTAL DOUBLE ARM-SINGLE WRIST
SEIZURE (level ground and elevated position)

Situation: A frontal assailant has captured your right wrist, clutching it rather firmly with both of his hands. He refuses to let go. You have limited space in which to move.

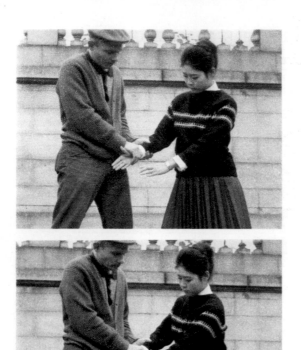

Response 1: At his grasp, keep your composure and balance. Quickly reach forward with your left hand, under the assailant's right arm. Clasp your hands tightly together. Tuck your chin in and brace yourself with a bit wider than normal stance. (See pictures above.)

Immediately upon clasping your hands together, step forward to a position between the assailant's feet, using your right foot, knee slightly bent. (See diagram.) As you step, shift your weight to your advanced right foot and pull your hands backward as you drive your right elbow forward to loosen his grasp. (See pictures next page.) Smash your right elbow hard into your assailant's solar plexus, or mid-section by continuing pulling your hands back and thrusting your elbow forward. This final striking action can be seen on page 44.

Key points: It may be necessary to take an initial adjustment step to get close enough to the assailant in order to clasp your hands together. You must do this to prevent bending forward at your hips and losing your balance. Keep upright as you clasp. Your release action is one continuous motion using your stepping and arm prying action against the assailant's grasp. Move away from him quickly after striking.

Response 2: If your assailant double-grasps your right wrist while you are in an elevated position such as on a stairway, quickly shift your weight to your highside foot (left shown) with that knee slightly bent. Keep your balance. (See upper picture.)

As the assailant pulls you in an attempt to bring you down to his level, quickly lift your right foot and bring that thigh parallel to the ground. Deliver a hard right foot edge straight into your assailant's knee (advanced one), groin, mid-section, or rib area. This final action can be seen on the next page.

Key points: This escape measure is similar to that shown in Response 3 on page 23. However, this situation is more dangerous and it is essential that you realize that the assailant's two-armed grasp gives him terrific pulling power to upset you. You must react very quickly and lean hard away from your opponent as you kick to counterbalance his pull. Be alert to use your left elbow or fist actions should the assailant pull you down. Move away quickly from him after kicking.

FRONTAL DOUBLE ARM-SINGLE WRIST
SEIZURE (alternate)

Situation: An assailant has loosely grasped your right wrist with both of his hands from the front. He refuses to release you. You have limited space to move around in.

Response 1: Ensure his loose grasp by keeping your composure. Do not tug to release yourself. Keeping your balance, quickly reach forward between the assailant's arms, passing your left hand over the assailant's right arm. Clasp your hands tightly together. (See pictures above.)

At your clasp, quickly step your right foot, knee slightly bent, to a position between the assailant's feet as shown in the diagram. Shift your weight to that foot as you pull back with both hands and drive your right elbow forward. (See pictures below.) Your elbow comes up and around from your right. Strike the assailant hard in his mid-section or rib area as you twist your body slightly to the left. This final action can be seen on top of page 50.

Response 2: Be calm and ensure his loose grasp by not tugging to release yourself. Pull your captured arm inward and rotate your wrist upward quickly, pressing the knife-edge of your captured hand hard against his right arm near his wrist. Simultaneously, shift your weight onto your right leg, keeping that knee slightly bent. Deliver a fast snap kick forward with your left foot into the assailant's right knee or shin most accessible to you. (See pictures above.)

Quickly return your leg, thigh parallel to the ground and step it directly backward. Plant it firmly on the ground. Simultaneously with this backward step, drive a fast Hand Spear hard into the assailant's facial area, using your left hand. (Pictures below.) This final action can be seen on the bottom of the next page.

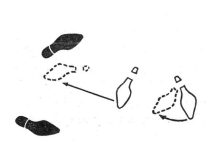

Key points: In Response 1, if your assailant grips hard, this escape may not work. Coordinate your weight shift, pulling, and hip twist with your striking actions. In Response 2, do not tug to release your captured arm, but use it for support as you kick. Coordinate your back step and Hand Spear action into one smooth movement. In either response, be alert to continue the defense. Break away as quickly as you can.

FRONTAL DOUBLE ARM-DOUBLE
WRIST SEIZURE

Situation: An assailant has grasped both your wrists, one in each of his hands, from the front. He is molesting you and refuses to let you alone. You have limited room to move around.

Response 1: Keep your composure and balance as the assailant grasps you. Bring your hands together with a quick motion as seen in the upper picture. Simultaneously, step your right foot between the assailant's legs as in the diagram and drive your right elbow hard into the assailant's mid section, passing over his left arm, and twisting your hips to the left as you do this. See lower picture and the final action on the next page.

Key points: If the assailant has a firm grip on your wrists, you can first attempt to spread your hands outward, making *him* force your hands together. Then suddenly reverse your exertion and snap your hands together. Coordinate your step, weight shift, and elbow striking action into one smooth movement. Keep alert for continuation of his attack. Break away quickly from him as he releases you.

53

Response 2: Keep your composure and balance at the assailant's grasp. Bring your hands together, passing your right hand under your left. (See picture to left.) As your right hand clears the other side of the assailant's right arm (outside), flex your right wrist so that the fingers point upward and the knife edge of that hand is pressed hard against the right wrist of the assailant. (See above right picture.) This action will loosen the assailant's grasp.

Continue pressing hard against the right wrist of your assailant with the knife edge of your right hand and immediately step backward with your right foot and twist your hips a bit to the right. Keep your weight centered on your left foot and do not place your right foot solidly on the ground unless absolutely necessary. This action will break your assailant's balance and weaken his grasp. (See pictures this page.) Quickly deliver a hard snap kick forward directly into the groin, knee, or shin of the assailant, using the tip of your right shoe or the ball of that foot. This final kicking action may be seen on the next page.

54

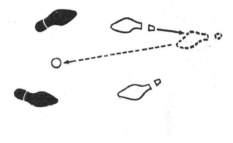

Key points: Similar to Response 1, if your assailant has taken a firm grasp, you can use the assailant's force to bring your hands together. Begin your resistance by trying to spread your hands apart, then as he resists, snap your hands together. The backward step with your right foot may be made at the time of passing your right hand under your left and as you press against the assailant's right wrist. The pressing must be hard as you coordinate this force with your kick. Be alert for repeated kicking if necessary and break away from the assailant as quickly as he releases you.

Response 3: Keep your composure and balance at the assailant's grasp. If he begins to pull you in toward him, quickly step your left foot backward to increase his pull. (See top and mid pictures and diagram.)

Keep your weight centered on your advanced right foot and do not allow your left foot to be planted solidly on the ground. (See middle picture.)

Immediately, deliver a hard Front Knee Kick direct to the assailant's groin, using your left leg and bringing it forward and upward fast from its rearward position. (See lowest picture.) This final kneeing action can be seen on the next page.

Key points: Do not struggle to release your hands. By keeping the assailant tied up in holding you, you have a perfect shot at the target area. Any pull he may make to bring you into him will increase the force of your kneeing action. Be sure not to bend forward too much as you take the short step backward. Break away quickly from him after kicking.

58

Chapter Two
PARTIAL BODY SEIZURES

AN attack by a single male assailant who has taken hold of a woman's body by grasping shoulders, neck, or garments is a more serious type of attack than those dealt with in Chapter One. It is often complicated by seizures which include the arms. This type of attack means closer contact with the assailant and concomitant danger. The assailant may have as his purpose, plain anger, robbery, or sexual lust, and his actions can include follow-up attacks by slapping, searching, liberties with her body, punching or striking, and even kneeing or kicking. Combinations of all these methods are often used in an attempt to gain the object of the attack.

Similarly, self-defense situations which involve you with an unarmed, single male assailant using these tactics in a standing position are obviously potentially dangerous situations in which an improper response on your part is almost sure to bring serious injury to you or the loss of your life.

A woman *highly* trained in *karate* technique can meet these situations but not without difficulty. If any of these situations happen to you, the average woman, you will be forced to defend yourself. The situations and the appropriate responses thereto, shown in this chapter, have been specifically selected for the average woman, and cover the necessary principles to successfully deal with common eventualities connected with unarmed single-assailant attacks in standing positions.

Practice all the responses with a partner. During your initial practices, begin slowly and gradually increase the speed of the attack and your response. Seek to build *automatic* responses. If you will practice a few

59

minutes a day, several days a week, this development will be greatly aided.

Perform all your actions in normal daily dress. Do not make the mistake of practicing only on a smooth, flat surface such as a gym floor, but try to make these responses on grass, gravel, paved and unpaved surfaces. This will bring you closer to reality—the situations as they could really happen. The responses of this chapter are given in terms of one side, either on the right or left, but in most cases the other side may and should be learned by simply reversing the instructions.

Some advice concerning your execution of the responses may prove helpful. Everything mentioned in Chapter 1 concerning your responses holds true here. But, expect tactics such as shown in this chapter to be made rather impulsively rather than with the "soft" approach. This means that you will have less time in which to demonstrate and convince your assailant that you will "cooperate" with him. In fact, you may get no chance to do this at all. You must rely upon speed of execution in your response without any prelude to it.

FRONTAL SINGLE ARM SHOULDER OR
GARMENT SEIZURE

Situation: A frontal assailant has laid a restraining hand on your left shoulder or has gripped your garment in the approximate area of your left shoulder. He is molesting you. You have plenty of room to move around.

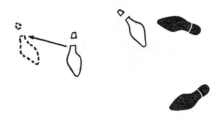

Response 1: Keep your composure and balance, but quickly step back a short step with your right foot as shown in the diagram. Swing your right arm up from behind and around across your assailant's face, *from the right,* keeping your hand open, palm down, fingers extended and joined. (See top pictures.)

62

Rake your fingers just across the front of his face near his eyes taking care that the arc-swing of your right arm is not too fast. If you do this too quickly, your assailant will not notice your action. He must *see* the raking action of your right hand. This will make him jerk his head back out of range to protect his eyes. Do not try to hit his face, merely rake across his face. Scratch him if you can. (See top picture.)

63

Allow your right arm swing to carry your right arm across to your left side. Fold your right arm across your upper body and bring your right hand, now formed into as tight fist, knuckles upward, near your left shoulder. Immediately deliver a hard stinging Back or Bottom Fist to the assailant's facial area by snapping your right arm forward into the target and twisting your hips in the direction of your striking action. (See pictures across the top of these two pages.) This final action can be seen on page 66.

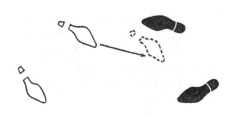

Response 2: Keeping your composure and balance, if your assailant uses his right hand grasp to pull you in closer to him, do not struggle to break away. Take advantage of his pull and step in quickly with left foot to a position between his feet. (See diagram.) Form both your fists tightly and deliver both of them simultaneously as you step. Drive them hard, the right fist into the assailant's facial area, and the left fist into his solar plexus, mid-section, or groin. (See pictures below.) This final action can be seen on the next page.

Key points: In Response 1, the arc-swing of your right hand is made effective by allowing your hips to twist to the left. It is a big motion. Likewise, your striking action is made in cooperation with your hips retwisting to the right. In Response 2, you must blend your step in action and your striking with the assailant's pull. Get there *faster* than he expected for best effect. When you strike with this double action, lean your body a bit into the assailant. Keep your left elbow close to your body as you strike. Get away from him quickly after striking.

FRONTAL ROBBERY THREAT

Situation: A frontal assailant has grasped your right shoulder, neck, or garments near your right shoulder with his left hand. He is threatening you and has demanded your purse. You have plenty of room to maneuver.

Response: Keep your composure and balance as he threatens you. However, you may lean away from him a bit, but do not struggle to break away. *Give* him your purse. (See top pictures.)

Watch the assailant carefully as he takes your purse and then go into action.

While he is taking the purse, step forward with your right foot, to a position just outside of his advanced left foot, turning your toes so that they point in toward his left foot. Leave your left foot in place. Simultaneously with this stepping action, perform a hard Rising Block, using your right arm, hard upward against the assailant's restraining left arm at any point along its underside. At the same time, withdraw your left arm alongside of your left side, hand in a tight fist, knuckles down. (See diagram and picture next page.)

Using your left arm, deliver a hard Elbow Forward Strike directly into the assailant's solar plexus, midsection, or groin, by quickly twisting your hips to your right and lunging forward into the assailant. This final action can be seen on the next page.

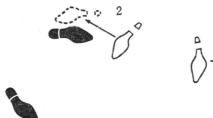

Key points: You must time your stepping, Rising Block, and left arm withdrawal in harmony at the time the assailant's mind is transferred from threatening you to receiving your purse. Premature action may spoil your chance. If the distance between you is too great, catch hold of the assailant's attacking left arm immediately after your Rising Block and hold on to it for support as you deliver a hard Foot Edge into the knee or shin of your assailant (see lower picture). Break away from him quickly after striking or kicking.

SIDE HOOKED-ARM SEIZURE

Situation: An assailant is molesting you from the side by hooking his left arm under yours and trying to pull you to him or get you to go along with him. You have little room to move.

Response: Keep your composure and balance. Quickly stamp a hard Foot Edge or heel into the assailant's advanced left foot by driving your right foot hard downward starting from a position well up on his shin and in contact with it. (See upper picture.)

72

Immediately, step your right foot behind the assailant's left foot as shown in the diagram and swing your right arm against his left side near his shoulder. Push hard toward his rear with your right hand to unbalance him as you withdraw your left arm alongside of your left hip, hand held in a tight fist, knuckles down. (See upper pictures.)

Deliver a smashing hard left Elbow Forward Strike directly into your assailant's solar plexus or midsection by using your left arm and twisting your body to the right as you strike. This final action can be seen on the next page.

Key points: Speed is essential in this action. Your initial stamping action causes intense pain and will weaken his grasp on you and his intentions. When you step and pivot your body, you must push hard with your right hand to unbalance him. Coordinate your step, hand push, hip twist, and striking actions into a smooth movement. Be alert for other opportunities such as kneeing him if necessary. Break away from him quickly when you finish your attack.

74

REAR GARMENT AND ARM SEIZURE

Situation: An assailant has come up behind you and is threatening to rob you. He grips your left wrist and has his right hand on your right shoulder and is attempting to push-pull and spin-turn you around so he can get at your purse. You have a limited space in which to move.

Response 1: As the assailant pushes your right shoulder and lift-pulls your left arm backwards in an attempt to turn you around, keep your composure and balance. Blend with his actions and do not tug to release yourself. Come around in the direction he is forcing you, but pivot your right foot a bit to your left and step your left foot in between his feet as shown in the diagram. Simultaneously, raise your captured left arm, flexing your wrist so that your fingers point upward and you are able to press hard against the assailant's left arm with the knife-edge of your hand. (See picture.)

Follow through by twisting your hips fast to your left, driving your right arm as a hard Elbow Forward Strike directly into the assailant's solar plexus or mid-section. (See pictures above.) The final striking-action can be seen on page 78.

76

Response 2: Keep your composure and balance as the assailant pulls you backward. Blend with his actions and do not tug forward. Come backward with his efforts by stepping your right leg directly backward between his feet. *Drop* your purse as you do this. Simultaneously raise your free right arm, hand held in a tight fist, knuckles upward, across your body so that your right fist is near your left shoulder. (See lower diagram and pictures.)

Simultaneously with your stepping backward, come around fast by twisting your hips to the right and drive a smashing right Elbow Rear Strike directly into your assailant's solar plexus, mid-section, or groin. The final striking action can be seen on the next page.

Key points: In either response, the key to successful counteraction is to blend with the assailant's force. Let him push you or pull you to spin you around, but come around *faster* than he expects. Be alert for other opportunities. In Response 1, as you turn to face him, if the distance is too great for an elbow strike, use a snap kick or kneeing action. In Response 2, as you are pulled back, if the distance is too great to use your elbow action, use a Foot Edge or heel attack. Break away from him as quickly as you can.

78

REAR CHOKING SEIZURE

Situation: You have suddenly been surprised by an assailant from behind. He has grabbed you by the neck in an effort to choke you or pull you backwards. You have very little room in which to move.

Response: Keep your composure and balance at all costs. As long as his hands are occupied in holding you, you have a fine chance to deliver an effective escape attack.

Tense your neck muscles if he is choking and immediately come around fast to your right. Keep your feet in place, but they may pivot a bit to aid your balance. Twist your hips hard to your right as you deliver a smashing Knife-hand or Bottom Fist directly to his groin. Watch your striking action. (See pictures top of these pages.)

Immediately, twist hard and fast to the other side (left) shown, still keeping your feet in place. As you twist, raise your left arm across your body, hand held in a tight fist near your mid-chest, knuckles outward. (Lowest picture.)

Deliver a hard left Elbow Rear Strike directly into the assailant's solar plexus, mid-section, or groin, passing below his attacking left arm. This final striking action can be seen on the next page.

Key points: Speed is essential in this response. Any delay may mean a more severe choking attack by the assailant. Both your right side and left side striking attacks must be done with a hard twist of your body to those sides in coordination with your striking arms.

Drop your hips a bit and brace your legs as you deliver these actions. After striking, move away from him as quickly as you can.

82

REAR ARM SEIZURE AND MUGGING.

Situation: An assailant has taken you into an attack from behind. He has encircled your neck with his right arm in an attempt to restrain you or choke you, while his left hand has grasped your left hand or wrist. He has drawn you up close to him and is bending you backwards. You have plenty of room to maneuver.

Response: It is essential to keep your composure. Your balance is being destroyed backward, so any struggle you make must be primarily designed to right yourself. Do not tug to get away for you are in a very weak position.

When you have righted your posture somewhat, drive a hard and fast foot heel straight down into the assailant's advanced right foot, using your right foot. (See picture and sketch above.)

Quickly take advantage of his momentary surprise by stepping your right foot backward to a position outside of his right foot. (See diagram.) Raise your right arm, bringing it forward, hand held open or in a tight fist. (Picture above.)

Drop your hips a bit and deliver a stinging hard and fast right Elbow Rear Strike straight into the assailant's solar-plexus, midsection, groin, or rib area, twisting your body into the direction of the strike. As your arm strikes, it rotates so that your hand comes to rest, knuckles down. This final striking action can be seen on the next page.

Key points: This rear attack is very dangerous to you, and any miscalculation on your part may eliminate your last chance to escape. It may be necessary to make repeated foot heel attacks initially before you step. When you step, twist fast and do not hesitate to strike with your elbow. Break away from him as quickly as you can.

86

Chapter Three
FULL EMBRACE SEIZURES

BY these attacks the self-appointed "Don Juan" assailant usually has the specific purpose of making advances to and taking sexual liberties with the female body. His initial approach may be either impulsive or "soft," but more often than not it begins "soft" and aims at restraining her so that he may talk her into consenting to his purpose. Nevertheless, these attacks can sometimes develop into complex situations involving anger and robbery when the assailant's amorous intentions are foiled by an uncooperative female. Follow up actions in these cases include slapping, punching or striking, and even kneeing or kicking, either separately or in combination with one another.

Self-defense situations which involve you with an unarmed, single male assailant, using these tactics against you in a standing position, are obviously all delicate situations in which the improper response by you may bring serious consequences.

Women highly trained in *karate* technique are able to face these situations with confidence, yet you, as an average female, cannot safely cope with them without some practical self-defense knowledge. The situations and the appropriate responses thereto, shown in this chapter, have been specially selected for you and cover the necessary principles to successfully deal with common eventualities connected with unarmed single-assailant attacks in standing positions.

Practice all the responses with a partner. During your initial practices begin slowly and gradually increase the speed of the attack and your response. Seek to build *automatic* responses. If you will practice a few minutes a day, several days a week, this development will be greatly aided.

Perform all your actions in normal daily dress. Do not make the mistake of giving yourself the convenience of a flat surface such as a gym floor, but try to make these responses on grass, gravel, paved and unpaved surfaces. This will bring you closer to reality—the situations as they could really happen.

The responses of this chapter are given in terms of one side, either on the right or left, but in most instances the other side may and should be learned by simply reversing the instructions.

Concerning your execution of the responses in this chapter, everything that has been mentioned in Chapter One holds true here, but it is necessary to expand that a bit so that you may more clearly realize the seriousness of it all.

There is an old saying, "when rape is inevitable, relax and enjoy it." This is especially true in self-defense situations, but we hasten to add—"up to a point." The assailant, using the full embrace type of attack, usually has only one purpose in mind—*he sexually wants your body*. As repugnant as this may be to you, your composure at the moment of his attack is essential to your safety. Your appearance of cooperation gives you the best chance of escaping from him. It is "*amour*" which is your weapon at the onset of his attack. Let him come closer; let him whisper "sweet nothings;" let him steal a kiss or two or obtain the "feel" he is after. It will be a small price to pay to ensure your escape which may not become possible at all if you insist on making wild, premature useless actions. These meaningless movements on your part will probably only anger him and cause him to use superior physical force to subdue you before he completes his attack. You have thus gained nothing but a very temporary delay. By appearing to melt in his embrace, you can cause his mind, which began with the idea of *amour*, but which was a bit wary of your possible resistance, to be convinced by your response. He thus loses all thoughts of anything but your body which is "welcoming" him. When he becomes passionately engrossed—cool him off fast by blasting him with everything you can muster behind a well-executed *karate* response.

SIDE EMBRACE

Situation: An amorous but objectionable assailant is molesting you by embracing you from the side. He has placed his left arm around your waist and is lightly holding your left arm. You are both half leaning against a railing, standing, or walking along. He refuses to release you. There is plenty of room to move about in.

Response: Keep your composure and do not struggle wildly to break away. By so doing, you may anger him and get him to tighten his grip, making your escape more difficult. Let him remain alongside of you. It is at this time that your best weapon is "amour" in the form of apparent "cooperation."

Seek to time your coming escape actions with the moment he is most intent on "conquering" you. *You* must provide him with that moment. If he tries to kiss you or make other advances to you, throw him mentally off guard by slowly "giving in." As he moves in for "greater things," you may begin your physical escape by stamping your right foot heel hard into his arch (either of his feet will do). (See sketch.)

Immediately follow this up with a hard striking action using your right elbow by bringing your arm up forcibly under his chin. This action may be seen in the above picture.

If the assailant has captured your right arm or hand as he embraces you, you may under similar circumstances, swing your left arm, hand held in a tight fist, up into his face from below, twisting your body a bit to the right as you do this. This final action may be seen on the next page.

Key points: The success of this simple situation from the escape stand-point depends upon your "acting" the part of a slowly "cooperating" receiver of his advances.

Premature actions on your part may complicate the situation and result in bodily harm to you. Be alert for continuation of his attentions and break away from him immediately upon striking.

FRONTAL EMBRACE ATTEMPT

Situation: You have been accosted by a tall, amorous assailant who is making advances to you. He holds you close to him somewhat frontally, his hands resting on your shoulders or arms to keep you from moving away. You have plenty of room to move around.

Response 1: At his grasp, keep your composure and act the part of thinking about "surrender." Run your arms around his waist a bit, he will think it "romance" and further unbalance himself mentally; but this action is to provide only balance support for your coming escape actions.

Quickly swing your right leg forward and bring it back pendulum like hard against the assailant's shin (left shown), using your heel as the striking point. (See pictures this page.)

Pivot quickly on your left foot and face into your assailant. (See diagram.) Immediately bring your left leg upward and deliver a hard smashing Front Knee Kick directly into his groin as your hands pull the assailant forward into your kneeing action. This action may be seen on the next page.

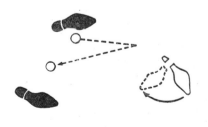

Response 2: If the situation is a bit modified in that the assailant has faced you and run his arms around your body under your arms (this position may also result from an ineffective Response 1), allow him to pull you in close, but raise your both arms sidewards, hands forming a tight fist with an extended middle finger knuckle and repeatedly jab him in the rib areas on each side of his body. (See picture above and sketch bottom of page 95.)

If your assailant does not release you with these measures, and, providing he is not too tall, use the same action of your hands, formed similarly, against his facial or head areas especially his temples. (See pictures this page.) This will loosen his grasp on you. Take advantage of his loose holding and twist inside of his arms as you deliver a hard smashing Elbow Forward Strike to his jaw. Either side will do (right elbow shown). This action can be seen on the next page.

Key points: Both of these responses demand you to "act" the part of "surrender" to his advances. In Response 1, your initial pendulum action of your right leg not only provides a striking force against your assailant's shin, but aids you to twist your body around to face him. Keep your left knee slightly bent as you knee him. Don't come up on your toes when kneeing him. If he is too tall, you may strike his groin with either fist. In Response 2, your final elbow strike is reinforced by clasping your hands together as you strike. Break away from him as quickly as you can.

FRONTAL EMBRACE (alternate)

Situation: An assailant of about your height has placed his arms around you, clasped them behind you, and is making advances which you find objectionable. He has pulled you in close to him and is preparing to kiss you. You have some room to move around.

99

Response: Here too, you must keep your composure and make the assailant think that you are about to "surrender." Put your arms around his waist to encourage this kind of thinking on his part. Quickly shift your weight to your slightly bent right leg and bring your left knee hard upward as a Forward Knee Kick directly into his groin, using your hands to pull him into it. (See upper picture.)

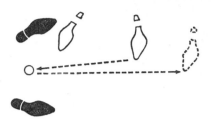

Quickly drop your arms from around his waist and bring your kicking left leg down by stepping backward as shown in the diagram at the top of the next page.

Simultaneously with your back step bring your left elbow upward as an Elbow Upward Strike and drive it hard into the jaw of your assailant. Twist your body to the right as you deliver it. This can be seen in the pictures at the bottom of this page. The final action can be seen on the next page.

Key points: Getting your assailant mentally off balance is essential and best accomplished by acting as if you enjoy his advances. Bring your elbow upward in a straight line; do not loop it. Be alert to use more kneeing action if necessary and break away from him as quickly as you can.

Situation: An amorously bent assailant has backed you up against a wall or a railing and has trapped you inside of his arms solidly placed on each side of you. He is pressing up close to you and is about to kiss you. There is little room to move.

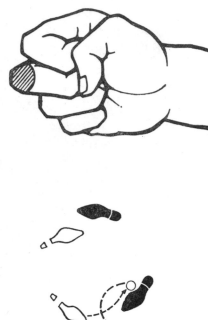

Response: Keep your composure, but go into action before your assailant closes in too tightly upon you. Use either fist or both fists with an extended mid-finger knuckle, to attack his exposed ribs and a hard heel kick using either leg (right shown) directly into his shin or lower leg areas. If you do this speedily and with good force, the assailant will loosen up his arm positions a bit. (See sketch and above picture.)

Step your kicking leg wide (to the right shown) and drop your hips a bit to make a bigger gap between you and your assailant. Simultaneously, swing your bent right arm in the form of a Elbow Forward Strike hard into the rib area of the assailant and follow it with an immediate Elbow Upward Strike, using your left arm directly under the assailant's jaw. (See pictures at the top of this page.) The final striking action can be seen on the next page.

Key points: Your initial fist and heel kicking attacks are designed to loosen your assailant's balance and to widen the distance between you. Repeated striking may be necessary. Be sure to drop your hips as you stop wide preparatory to your elbow-striking actions. Break away from him as quickly as you can after striking.

Situation: An amorous assailant has placed his arms around you, over both of your arms, from behind. He clasps his hands in front of you, and is holding you loosely in an effort to make advances to you. You have enough room to move around.

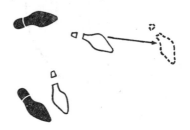

Response 1: You must keep your composure and make him think that you are considering "surrender." Make your escape quickly by stepping forward with your left foot in a slightly longer-than-normal step as shown in the diagram. As you step, swing both of your arms upward directly in front of you and bend your knees to lower your body a bit (left picture). This action will free you from his rear grasp.

Quickly twist your body to your right rear and deliver a hard right Elbow Rear Strike straight into your assailant's solar plexus, midsection, or groin as you withdraw your left arm along your left side, hand held in a tight fist, knuckles down, at your left hip. (See right picture.) This final action can be seen on the next page (left picture).

Key points: It is essential that you snap your body forward into the step, bending your knees a bit, dropping your shoulders as you fling your arms forward and upward quickly. This is a dip-step of your body which *hollows* your chest, not raises it. Coordinate your body twist with the motion of your elbow striking. Sometimes if your stepping is badly executed or if your assailant reacts suddenly to pull you back to him before you can make your elbow strike you will be able to chop a hard right knife-edge into his groin as he pulls you back (right picture). Be alert for other opportunities and break away from him as quickly as you can.

Response 2: Your composure here too is necessary to keep your assailant holding you lightly. Quietly bring your hands together, pressing your palms in front of you (upper picture). Suddenly drop your hips straight down by stepping your right foot a bit backward between your assailant's feet and bending your knees. (See diagram.) Drive your arms hard upward against the undersides of his. This action will loosen his light grasp. Immediately, drive a hard right Elbow Rear Strike into his solar plexus, midsection, or groin. This action can be seen in the lower picture.

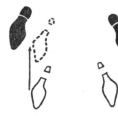

Key points: You must drop your body straight down quickly. Do not put your buttocks backward. Repeated elbow striking may be necessary. Break away from your assailant as quickly as you can.

Response 3: This response may be necessary if Responses 1 and 2 have failed, or if for any reason your assailant has tightened his hold on you. He may even have grabbed your left arm in front of your body. Go immediately into action by driving a hard right foot heel straight down into his right instep. (See upper left picture.) Quickly step your right foot wide to the right and outside of his right foot as shown in the diagram.

Bend your knees as you step and fling your arm hard upward to loosen his grasp. (See right picture.) Slip your hips a bit to the right and then rapidly twist your body to your left and deliver a hard left Bottom Fist or Knife-hand straight into his groin. This final action can be seen on the next page.

Key points: You must step wide and drop rapidly as you fling your arms upward to loosen his grasp. If you are unable to slip your hips to the right to make your Bottom Fist or Knife-hand possible, use your left Elbow Rear Strike into his solar plexus, mid-section, or groin. Break away quickly from him after striking.

Situation: An amorous assailant holds you rather tightly around your waist, under your both arms, from behind. He has clasped his hands in front of you and is attempting to make further advances to you. You have plenty of room in which to move.

Response 1: Keep your composure and quietly make tight fists of both your hands. Check which of the assailant's hands is uppermost (right shown). You will attack with your fist on this same side (right). Form that fist with the knuckle of your middle finger extended as shown in the sketch. Go into action by driving the extended knuckle of your right hand hard into the assailant's right hand top surface. He will release his hand clasp and loosen his hold on you. (See top pictures.)

Quickly take advantage of this lack of restraint to step forward away from him by advancing your left foot and sliding your right foot forward taking care to point your toes to your right as shown in the diagram. This action prepares you for the next striking action.

Immediately twist your body fast to your right and drive a hard right Elbow Sideward Strike into your assailant's solar plexus, midsection, or groin. As you do this, withdraw your left arm alongside of your left side, hand formed as a tight fist, knuckles down. This final striking action can be seen on the next page.

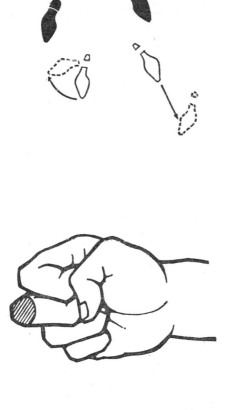

Key points: When you release yourself from the assailant, you may terminate your striking at this point depending upon circumstances. Sometimes if the assailant does not follow you forward or steps back at the shock of your fist knuckle attack, it will be impossible for you to deliver an effective elbow striking action. In this case you may turn more to face him and use a snap kick to his groin, knee, or shin, using your left shoe tip or ball of that foot.

Response 2: Providing that your assailant is not too tall, you may go into action by butting the back of your head hard against his facial areas. (See top picture.)

Immediately follow this action by a hard stamping action using your right foot heel directly downward into his right instep. (See sketch.) These combined actions, butting and heel striking, will loosen the assailant's grip on you and give you an opportunity to turn away from him (lower picture). Do this by quickly stepping your right foot circularly forward, toes pointing to your left and pivoting to your left as shown in the diagram.

Simultaneously with your left turn, deliver a hard left Elbow Sideward Strike up into his facial area, coming up in a swinging motion as fast as you can. Withdraw your right arm alongside of your body, hand held in a tight fist, knuckles down, at your right hip. This final striking action can be seen in the picture on the next page.

Key points: Repeated butting and heel kicking may be necessary. You may also use the extended knuckle of your tight fist into his uppermost top hand surface as you did in Response 1. Be alert to deal with any continuation of his attack against you.